David McCord

Holt, Rinehart and Winston

New York Toronto London Sydney

A Satellite Book

Satellite Books are supplementary units designed for
individualized, independent reading to accompany
THE HOLT BASIC READING SYSTEM, by Bernard J. Weiss
and Lyman C. Hunt.

General Editors
SATELLITE BOOKS

Lyman C. Hunt
Patricia Hynes Estill

Grateful acknowledgement is given to the following
publisher and author: Little, Brown and Company, Boston,
for "Couplet," "Quatrain," "Limerick," and "Triolet," from
Take Sky, copyright © 1961 and © 1962 by David McCord.
Used by permission.

The author is grateful to Arthur Thornhill, Jr., and Miss
Helen Jones of Little, Brown and Company for making some
of his earlier poems available for this book.

Contents

Dear Reader,

This book is about poetry. It is not about the great poetry of the past, nor is it about the great poetry of the present. It is about the first steps to take in learning the art of writing poetry, or, for that matter, the first steps to take in the art of learning to read and understand poetry.

No poet worth his salt has ever been able to write the kinds of poems he wanted to write without a basic knowledge of meter, rhythm, rhyme, and the established verse forms. A good poet must be very sensitive to words. He must understand the relation of words to each other, how they sound together, and how they react to, and on, each other. A poet may decide to abandon the use of rhyme, which many poets do not like or use, because rhyme is not really essential. He may abandon most of the classic verse forms, but he will never abandon meter and rhythm. A true poet is a writer who can *hear* the dreadful sound of collision when a wrong word strikes a right word. If a writer does not have the art of placing words that sound and work together in the proper meter and rhythm, he may write till the cows come home, but he will *not* be writing poetry.

In this book I shall be talking almost entirely about verse form, and I shall discuss each form by using the form I am writing about. This is because I should like each verse form to come alive for you *at the instant* you meet it. If you were to tell me how to make and fly a kite, or how to knit a sweater, it would be much better if we actually had a kite or a sweater to work on, wouldn't

4

it? So I can better show you how to write a limerick by writing one for you than by just telling you about it.

It may surprise you to see that each verse form has so many rules which must be followed. The rules are not hard. In some cases they are extremely simple. Try not to break the rules; if you do, you are cheating. You will not be cheating me or your teacher or poetry; you will be cheating yourself. Say to yourself: This is the way the great poets learned to write poetry — by studying and practicing such forms as these. If you try hard enough, you will master them.

I fully understand that you may not want to become a poet. A true poet is born with the gift, and there is no point in worrying about it if you lack the gift. But here is a chance for you to look through many different doors at a way of expressing certain rhythms of art through the basic rhythms of our English language. You *do* speak English, and you *do* try to write it, and learning how to write poetry is the surest and quickest way to achieve a mastery over both speaking and writing that will help you all your life.

Small as these first steps in the world of poetry may seem to be, wait till you have written, say, one really good haiku or triolet! I think you will suddenly discover how much satisfaction you can have just because you followed the rules and achieved something nearly perfect all by yourself. So if you will get some paper and a pen, we can tackle these poems together.

David Reshard

Couplet

1

A couplet is two lines — two lines in rhyme.
The first comes easy, the second may take time.

2

Most couplets will have lines of equal length;
This gives them double dignity and strength.

3

Please count the syllables in 2 and say
How many. Ten each line? Correct! And they

4

In turn comprise the five-foot standard line:
Pentameter. The foot's *iambic*. Fine

5

Enough! On human feet, of course, our shoes
Do match; likewise the laces. If you choose

6

A briefer line,
Like this of mine,

7

Or say
O.K.,

8

Why, *these* are couplets, somewhat crude but true
To form. Try one yourself. See how you do.

The Couplet as a Stanza

1

The couplet has another role.
What is it, then, if not a whole

two-line complete affair? Why, it's
a stanza. One by one it fits

into a poem of any size.
These couplets, spaced like railroad ties,

well ballasted, precise and true,
permit the poem *to pass right through* —

not *over* them. The reader feels
he's having one fine ride on wheels.

2

The couplet, in effect, thus runs
a *little* poem along, *great guns*,

but tends to slow the reader when
the couplets number more than ten.

Five, six, or seven seem to be
enough. At least they are for me.

Well, here's a poem that speaks of snails,
and yet I do not think it fails

to move at quite a lively pace,
not losing much of snail-like grace.

3

The snail is slow. The swift gazelle
could never manage with a shell.

The snail, without his shell, would squirm
and look a lot like half a worm.

To find him, you would need to peek
inside some nasty robin's beak.

The poor gazelle must run to stay
alive. And that's about the way

it is with snails and swift gazelles:
some have, and some do not have, shells.

Quatrain

1

When there is more to say — or more than planned —
A couplet's very easy to expand.
Expansive couplets, then, if out of hand,
May nicely run to four lines. Understand?

2

Four lines — quatrain; long lines or short,
But *good* lines, with a good report
Of one another as they progress.
Note: óne / an óth / er for chánge / of stréss

3

Or emphasis: the sudden sharpening pace.
A quatrain says its say with perfect grace.
"I strove with none, for none was worth my strife" —
First line of four* to haunt you all your life.

4

I'll not attempt a long example —
I mean with lines of many feet;
But still you ought to have a sample
Or two to prove the form *is* neat.

*See Walter Savage Landor in *Bartlett's Familiar Quotations*.

5

Here goes:
Suppose
Suppose
Suppose

6

The ship sails for Spain,
For Spain the ship sails;
You can't go by train,
For a train runs on rails.

7

Let's sail a ship for far-off Spain;
We really can't get there by train.
But still a big ship has no sails;
Why not a train that has no rails?

8

Note rimes in 1 — the rime* control is *planned*.
In 2, *two* pairs of rimes; in 6 we find
a-b-a-b (*Spain, sails, train, rails*). Last kind
Is this (a-b-b-a): *planned, find, kind, and* —

9

Forget that ship that has no sails.
Let's jet by plane across to Spain
Above the sea they call the Main.
(Say something here that rimes with *sails*.)

*Note: I am spelling *rhyme* the short way — *rime*.

11

The Quatrain as a Stanza

1

The quatrain is a common stanza form,
And half the poems you know have used it. Much
Of nonsense verse, departing from the norm,
Is one quatrain, or two, or many such.

Some funny epitaphs are one quatrain.
Quatrains are fine for packaged silliness.
Why this is so, I really can't explain.
Have I a nonsense poem? How did you guess!

I have. And while I'm at it, I advise:
When you have read it, try to write a bit
Of nonsense in quatrains. It may surprise
You what this stanza form will do for it.

2

The clouds are full of new blue sky,
The water's full of sea;
The apple's full of deep-dish pie,
And I am full of me.

My money's full of pockets, too,
My teeth are full of jaw;
The animals are full of zoo,
The cole is full of slaw.

How full things are of this and that:
The tea so full of spoon;
The wurst so *very* full of brat;
The shine, brimful of moon.

Limerick

1

A limerick shapes to the eye
Like a small very squat butterfly,
    With its wings open wide,
    Lots of nectar inside,
And a terrible urge to fly high.

2

The limerick's lively to write:
Five lines to it — all nice and tight.
    Two long ones, two trick
    Little short ones; then quick
As a flash here's the last one in sight.

3

Some limericks — most of them, reely —
Make rimes fit some key word like *Greely*
    (A man) of *Dubuque*
    (Rimed with cucumber — *cuque*)
Or a Sealyham (dog). Here it's *Seely*.

4

There once was a scarecrow named Joel
Who couldn't scare crows, save his soel.
    But the crows put the scare
    Into Joel. He's not there
Any more. That's his hat on the poel.

5

"There was an old man" of wherever
You like, thus the limerick never
    Accounts for the young:
    You will find him unsung
Whether stupid, wise, foolish, or clever.

6

There was a young man, let me say,
Of West Pumpkinville, Maine, U.S.A.
    You tell me there's not
    Such a place? Thanks a lot.
I forget what he did anyway.

7

Take the curious case of Tom Pettigrew
And Hetty, his sister. When Hettigrew
    As tall as a tree,
    She came just to Tom's knee.
And did *Tom* keep on growing? You bettigrew.

8

Consider this odd little snail
Who lives on the rim of a pail:
    Often wet, never drowned,
    He is always around
Safe and sound, sticking tight to his trail.

9

A man who was fond of his skunk
Thought he smelled pure and pungent as punk.
    But his friends cried No, no,
      No, no, no, no, no, *no!*
He just stinks, or he stank, or he stunk.

10

There was an old man who cried Boo!
Not to me or to he but to you.
    He also said scat
    To a dog not a cat,
And to Timbuc he added too-too.

11

It's been a bad year for the moles
Who live just in stockings with holes;
    And bad for the mice
    Who prefer their boiled rice
Served in shoes that don't have any soles.

12

There once was a man in the Moon,
But he got there a little too soon.
    Some others came later
    And fell down a crater —
When *was* it? Next August? Last June?

13

"This season our 'tunnips' was red,
And them beets was all white. And instead
    Of green cabbages, what
    You suspect that we got?"
"I don't know." "Didn't plant none," he said.

14

I don't much exactly quite care
For these cats with short ears and long hair;
    But if anything's worse
    It's the very reverse:
Just you ask any mouse anywhere.

15

So by chance it may be you've not heard
Of a small sort of queer silent bird.
    Not a song, trill, or note
    Ever comes from his throat.
If it does, I take back every word.

16

Write a limerick now. Say, "There was
An old man" of some place, what he does,
    Or perhaps what he doesn't,
    Or isn't or wasn't.
Want help with it? Give me a buzz.

Clerihew

1

The clerihew
Is a tricky form for you.
The first two lines state a fact;
The second two, how you react.

2

Perhaps a name,
Then a line describing the same.
You take off from there.
What you say is your own affair.

3

Samson, you might say,
Had long hair for his day.
What horrid thoughts we harbor
For the first lady barber!

4

Babe Ruth
Is a legend now to youth.
I saw the Babe in action,
Which was a greater satisfaction.

5

One way to save gas
Is *not* to cut the grass.
Other ways there may be,
But this one saves me.

6

You can see the opening line
In these clerihews of mine
Can be long or short. The zip
In the short is *the crack of a whip*.

7

To the playground the mothers bring
Their children for a swing.
The mothers do the bringing
And also the swinging.

8

The Nottoway
Never got away
To the Platte away
Out thataway.

9

Cheyenne
Is sheer magic; but then,
So is Broken Bow,
Moosejaw, and Jump Off Joe.

10

The skunk
Has a lot of spunk.
If the reason isn't plain,
He will gladly explain.

11

When a rooster crows
Everybody knows
The dawn made him do it.
That's all there is to it.

12

The dolphin's brain
Is something we'd fain
Know a lot more about.
Not so the brain of a trout.

Haiku

1

Because it is short,
Japanese three-line haiku
   Almost writes itself.

2

Count the syllables!
Five each in lines one and three,
   Seven in line two.

3

Syllable writing,
Counting out your seventeen,
   Doesn't produce poem.

4

Good haiku need thought:
One simple statement followed
   By poet's comment.

5

Take the butterfly:
Nature works to produce him.
   Why doesn't he last?

6

Whistles in the night
Sound so far off and lonely.
   Are you blowing them?

7

Mackerel-shaped cloud
Means a hard rain very soon.
Mackerel will swim.

8

Frogs are comical:
A curious arrangement
Of eyes, mouth, flat feet.

9

The town dump is white
With seagulls, like butterflies
Over a garden.

10

In the laundromat
Dryer the Angels always
Seem to beat the Sox.

11

The big truck says, *No!*
Little VW says,
I'll pass. Yes, I *will!*

12

I like country roads
With bends in them. What is round
The bend? Don't tell me.

13

Imagination
Works like a marvelous dream
Which you can control.

Cinquain

1

This is
the form of the
cinquain. The five lines have
2, 4, 6, 8, 2 syllables,
as here.

2

Be / gin.
That's two / Two more
Now / six / syl / la / bles / and
then / eight / syl / la / bles / You / count / them
Now / two

3

No / rhymes
All / so / eas / y
Just / keep / count / cor / rect / ly
I'm / di / vid / ing / the / syl / la / bles
for / you

4

Let's build
something. Guess what?
A cellar first. A floor.
A ceiling. A roof over it.
A house.

5

Four paws,
four feet, head, tail,
two eyes, two ears, a mouth,
a good nose for smelling things. *What?*
A dog.

6

Pen, ink,
table, paper,
an idea, a first line,
more lines, changes, great long pauses:
a poem.

7

Behind
always behind
following after me
in the way   but still my little
brother

8

Everything
small   very small
neat   orderly   lifelike
real as the real thing   only small
Doll's House

9

A sound
far-off   haunting
You must listen quite close
else you won't hear it faintly roar
Sea shell

10

What lives
under water
very fierce   Eats small fish
then crawls on land to shed its skin
and fly?

11

Love all
rivers   They are
man's friend   ally   power
Near them he builds his cities   Keep
them clean

12

Do you
care for crickets?
I love their summer sound
Late fall I like one in a house
chirping

13

Raccoons
are surprising
Black mask   feet much like hands
They always seem to walk down hill
Rascals!

14

Have you
ever seen a
China piggy bank chock
full of pennies? *Absolutely*
full? No?

15

Try your
hand at cinquains.
They *show* their form, teach you
To be simple, direct, precise.
Are you?

Tercet

1

A tercet is a stanza of three lines,
All rhyming; like a pitchfork with three tines,
Or like three stars if none of them outshines

The others. Tercets have a natural grace,
And move along like this in easy pace,
And look up at you face to face to face.

But you can change the rhyme scheme as you wish.
When you go fishing and you bait your hook,
The thing you hope to catch, of course, is fish.

And so with writing tercets. Now I look
For some fresh other rhyme that I can squeeze
In there as with the *hook* and *look* I took

To brighten up this poem. Can a tercet breeze
Into the next this way? Well, so it seems.
Why not? If now we let this third line freeze,

We're back to where we started. On with *dreams!* —
An old poetic word at once redeems
Our one-rhyme scheme. I could go on for reams

Of paper, but I think by now you see
How pleasant tercets are to write. Write me,
Should you have trouble with them. Here I be.

2

I've looked behind the shed
And under every bed:
I think he must be dead.

What reason for alarm?
He doesn't know the farm.
I *knew* he'd come to harm!

He was a city one
Who never had begun
To think the city fun.

Now where could he have got?
He doesn't know a lot.
I haven't heard a shot.

That old abandoned well,
I thought. Perhaps he fell?
He didn't. I could tell.

Perhaps he found a scent:
A rabbit. Off he went.
He'll come back home all spent.

Groundhogs, they say, can fight;
And raccoons will at night.
He'd not know one by sight!

I've called and called his name.
I'll never be the same.
I blame myself . . . I blame . . . .

All *he* knows is the park;
And now it's growing dark.
A bark? *You hear a bark?*

Triolet

1

The triolet's droll;
You must watch it repeat
The lines in control.
The triolet's droll
With a brightness of soul,
With such swift little feet!
The triolet's droll;
You must watch it repeat.

2

The birds in the feeder
are fighting again.
Not squirrels in the cedar,
but birds in the feeder.
They haven't a leader:
just eight, nine, or ten
of the birds in the feeder
are fighting again.

3

The swallows all twitter
In line on the wire.
Each fatter and fitter,
The swallows all twitter:
Old sitter, young sitter,
Madame and Esquire.
The swallows all twitter
In line on the wire.

4

Eggs are all runny,
Though legs they have none.
It's terribly funny
That eggs are all runny!
When laid by a bunny
For Easter, not one
Of *his* eggs are all runny:
They roll and *we* run.

5

It's a foggy day
When winter thaws
And the snow is grey.
It's a foggy day:
O Doggy, go 'way
With your dirty paws!
It's a foggy day
When winter thaws.

6

I fed some cheese
To the cellar mice.
It went like a breeze
When I fed some cheese;
And they came by threes
And they came in a trice
When I fed some cheese
To the cellar mice.

Conclusion

Walking up the street,
Depressed and ill at ease,
And suffering from the heat
At 96 degrees,
With not a single breeze,
I think that I should warn:
It's just on days like these
A poem somehow is born.

Ah, wilderness! How meet!
A lake, canoe, big trees;
Mosquitoes, shredded wheat,
Canned milk, sardines, strong cheese;
Old sneakers, dungarees;
A pup tent badly torn.
Rain almost *guarantees*
A poem somehow is born!

Winter we dread to greet.
The water pipes will freeze,
The roads be slick with sleet,
The nose produce a sneeze.
We watch the late TV's,
Then lie awake, count shorn
Old sheep; but dream decrees
A poem somehow is born.

Some Rules about Meter and Rhyme

by Lyman C. Hunt

What Is Rhyme?

"A couplet is two lines — two lines in rhyme."

When two lines of verse have the very same sound at the very end, we say these lines rhyme. All the *couplets* in this book on pages 6 and 7 are examples of two lines of verse that rhyme.

When *four* lines of verse rhyme, we call this a *quatrain*. (See pages 10 and 11.) You can see that in a quatrain, all four lines do not have to use identical rhyme, although they sometimes do, as in the first quatrain on page 10.

At other times, a quatrain may be like two couplets joined together — the first two lines rhyme with each other, but line 3 rhymes only with line 4. Poets call this kind of quatrain an *a-a-b-b* rhyme. The letters *a-a* show that the first two lines have the same rhyme; the letters *b-b* show that the third and fourth lines have the same rhyme. You can learn all about this kind of quatrain if you look at the quatrains numbered 2 and 3 on page 10. Notice that each *clerihew* on pages 18 and 19 is also a quatrain with an *a-a-b-b* rhyme.

If you look at the last quatrain on page 10, you will see another kind of rhyme for a quatrain. It is called *a-b-a-b* rhyme. By now you know that the two *a*'s show that line 1 rhymes with line 3, and the two *b*'s show that lines 2 and 4 rhyme with each other.

And if you turn to page 11 and look at quatrains 8 and 9, you will find a kind of rhyme where the first line rhymes with the last line, and line 2 rhymes with line 3. That's easy to figure out: *a-b-b-a*.

This arrangement of the lines of a poem in different patterns of rhyme is called the *rhyme scheme*. It is the poet's rhyme plan for the poem.

Did you look carefully at the *triolet*? (See pages 28 and 29.) This poem has a very interesting rhyme scheme. It has eight lines which rhyme *a-b-a-a-a-b-a-b*. What is even more unusual about this verse form is that lines 1, 4, and 7 must repeat each other exactly, word for word; and line 8 must be exactly the same as line 2. The poet adheres strictly to these rules in triolets 1 and 3.

What Is a Stanza?

When any verse form is not used as a whole poem by itself, but is only a part of a longer poem, we call it a *stanza*. Usually, all the stanzas in a poem will have exactly the same rhyme scheme.

What Is Rhythm or Meter?

Rhyme is not the most important thing in a poem, though it does sound well. The poet, Louis Untermeyer, speaks of "the strong gongs of rhyme." But *rhythm* or *meter* is much more important. In a short essay he wrote about his life, David McCord says: "Rhythm, not rhyme, is the basis of poetry." He says his love of poetry came from "loving the sound of words and the rhythm of words put together in the right order."

Rhythm is a pattern of strong and weak sounds, like the upbeats and downbeats in music. Some of the beats are heavy and some are light. Rhythmic beats are the most important thing in poetry. In music these beats are called the *rhythm*, but in poetry they are usually called the *meter*.

The most common rhythm in English poetry is a meter with two beats, called *iambic* meter. It is one light beat followed by one heavy beat, like this:

$$- \ / \qquad \bar{e} \ / \ \text{noúgh} \qquad b\bar{e} \ / \ \text{liéve}$$

These two beats make one *iamb*, and are called a *metrical foot*. A line of verse can have any number of metrical feet from one to six, seven or more; but the usual number is five. Most of our best known poetry has five feet of iambic meter, like this:

$$- \ / - \ / - \ / - \ / - \ /$$

Mōst cóuplēts wíll hāve línes ōf équāl léngth.

There are ten beats altogether in this line, or ten syllables: five light beats, each followed by a heavy beat. This kind of verse is called *iambic pentameter*, which comes from the Greek word *penta*, meaning *five*. This is explained in poetic form on page 6.